PIANO · VOCAL · GUITAR

THE BRITISH INVASION
1964-1967

ISBN 0-7935-7904-X

HAL•LEONARD®
CORPORATION
7777 W. BLUEMOUND RD. P.O. BOX 13819 MILWAUKEE, WI 53213

Visit Hal Leonard Online at
www.halleonard.com

THE BRITISH INVASION

CONTENTS

4   Band Biographies

	SONG	ARTIST	YEAR
81	I'll Never Find Another You	The Seekers	1965
92	I'm a Man	The Yardbirds	1965
96	I'm a Man	The Spencer Davis Group	1967
100	I'm Into Something Good	Herman's Hermits	1964
106	Love Is All Around	The Troggs	1968
103	Love Potion Number 9	The Searchers	1964
110	Marie	The Bachelors	1965
114	Misery	The Beatles	1965
117	Mrs. Brown You've Got a Lovely Daughter	Herman's Hermits	1965
120	My Generation	The Who	1966
123	On a Carousel	The Hollies	1967
126	San Franciscan Nights	Eric Burdon & The Animals	1967
130	Stop Stop Stop	The Hollies	1966
136	There's a Kind of Hush	Herman's Hermits	1967
140	Ticket to Ride	The Beatles	1965
144	Time Is on My Side	The Rolling Stones	1964
147	True Love Ways	Peter & Gordon	1965
150	We Can Work It Out	The Beatles	1965
156	We Gotta Get Out of This Place	The Animals	1965
153	A Whiter Shade of Pale	Procol Harum	1967
160	Wild Thing	The Troggs	1966
163	Willow Weep for Me	Chad & Jeremy	1964
166	Wishin' and Hopin'	Dusty Springfield	1964
170	World without Love	Peter & Gordon	1964
173	You Really Got Me	The Kinks	1964

The Animals
(Eric Burdon & The Animals)

Shortly after Eric Burdon became the lead singer of The Alan Price Combo in 1962, the group renamed themselves The Animals. Formed in 1958 with Alan Price on keyboards, Bryan "Chas" Chandler on bass, John Steel on drums, and Hilton Valentine on guitar, the band already had a loyal following in its home town of Newcastle when Burdon signed on. The band's R&B-influenced style, and help from producer Mickie Most, won them a #1 hit in Britain and the U.S. with "House of the Rising Sun" (1964). The band continued scoring hits with tunes like "Don't Let Me Be Misunderstood" and "We Gotta Get Out of This Place" (both 1965). With Dave Rowberry replacing Price and Barry Jenkins replacing Steel, the group managed a few more hits, including "Don't Bring Me Down" (1966). After adding Eric Burdon's name to their billing, the group went psychedelic with "San Franciscan Nights" (1967). A few more hits and the band broke up. Burdon reappeared as Eric Burdon & The New Animals for a short time before pursuing solo work. After their breakup, the band reunited for a 1968 Christmas show at the Newcastle City Hall and recording sessions in 1976 (*Before We Were So Rudely Interrupted*) and 1983 (*Ark*). In 1992 they appeared in Moscow, performing in Red Square with an altered lineup. The Animals were inducted into the Rock and Roll Hall of Fame in 1994.

The Bachelors

There is a story that in the moments after Beatlemania began, every hotel room within shouting distance of Liverpool was filled with would-be agents and managers scouting for the next big Merseybeat act. According to legend, producer Shel Thalmy, who later introduced The Kinks, found three Irish harmonica players who wanted to learn to sing. Whether or not his assertions of having taught them to harmonize are true, the group did manage to place seventeen tunes, including "Marie" (1965), in the British Top Forty before disappearing in 1967.

THE BEATLES

The Beatles were undoubtedly the most important ensemble in the history of pop and rock music. As such, they exerted a profound social influence over a generation of young people. From their roots in skiffle (ad hoc, poor-man's bands of varying instrumentation) and R&B, the group created a British rock sound for the first time since American rock music had hit the British Isles. John Lennon was playing with his skiffle band, The Quarrymen, in 1957, when he met Paul McCartney. They teamed up and began writing songs together. Later that year George Harrison signed on, and the group's name was changed to Johnny and the Moondogs. Stu Sutcliffe, who could hardly play a note of music, joined the band, as did drummer Tommy Moore, and the name changed again to The Silver Beetles. It was soon shortened to The Beetles and then changed to The Beatles. Moore was replaced by Pete Best in 1960. Sutcliffe, who was the first of the group to sport the long, shaggy hair that started the Beatle haircut, left in 1961. The group cut their teeth in the red-light district of Hamburg. Brian Epstein found the group, cleaned them up a bit, and struggled to land them a record contract. In 1962 producer George Martin signed them with EMI Parlophone. Shortly afterwards, Best was replaced by drummer Ringo Starr. By early 1963 the group had scored several British hits and Beatlemania was in full swing in Britain. The album *Meet the Beatles* was introduced in the U.S. in January 1964 along with the group's fourth single, "I Want to Hold Your Hand." Both topped the U.S. charts. On February 7, 1964, The Beatles appeared on "The Ed Sullivan Show" to over 70 million Americans. The British Invasion had begun. Concerts, recordings, films, tours, and a constant flood of screaming fans followed that appearance. The group grew as musicians and by 1967 had ventured into what would be known as art rock. From the release of the album *Magical Mystery Tour* (1967), the group began pulling in separate directions. On April 10, 1970, Paul McCartney announced that The Beatles were finished. As each member pursued solo projects, finding varying degrees of success, fans clamored for a reunion. Reunion hopes were dashed in 1980 when John Lennon was killed by a mentally disturbed fan. The Beatles were inducted into the Rock and Roll Hall of Fame in 1988.

CHAD & JEREMY

A soft-rock folksy duo, Chad & Jeremy were a far greater success in America than in their native Britain. The pair—Chad Stuart on vocals, guitar, piano, sitar, tamboura, tabla, banjo, and flute, and Jeremy Clyde on vocals and guitar—were both well-educated and raised in wealthy circumstances. They met while studying acting at the Central School of Drama in Britain. Although they scored only one hit on the British charts, "Summer Song" (1964), their tunes, including "Yesterday's Gone" and "Willow Weep for Me" (both 1964), were almost constantly present on the U.S. charts from 1964 to 1966. Rivaling Peter & Gordon as the most popular early folk-rock duo, the pair were frequently seen on television shows, both musical and variety shows and series like "Batman." The duo broke up in 1966 when Clyde left to act in a West End production. They reunited in 1967 to record one of the first concept albums, *Of Cabbages and Kings*, and *The Ark*. After their final breakup in 1967, Clyde continued to act in theatre, film, and television. Stuart was music director for "The Smothers Brothers Comedy Hour" and continued to perform and compose musical comedies. In 1985 the pair appeared together in a West End production of *Pump Boys and Dinettes*.

THE DAVE CLARK FIVE

In 1964 The Dave Clark Five was briefly hailed as the only serious competition to The Beatles. As the first band of the British Invasion to follow The Beatles to the U.S., the group scored seventeen hits during the Invasion years of 1964–67. Band members Dave Clark on drums, Mike Smith on piano and vocals, Rick Huxley and Lenny Davidson on guitar, and Denis Payton on sax, were members of the Tottenham Hotspurs soccer team. They formed the band to raise money to play a match in Holland, eventually giving up soccer for music. With hits like "Glad All Over" and "Bits and Pieces" (both 1964), the group outdid The Beatles and most other bands in sheer decibel levels. The Dave Clark Five was the first British act to follow The Beatles on "The Ed Sullivan Show," eventually making a record eighteen appearances on the show. They were also seen in several films, including *Get Yourself a College Girl* (1964), *Lucy* (1965), and *Having a Wild Weekend* (1965). After the group ceased to score U.S. hits in 1968, they kept a following in Britain. They broke up in 1970. Clark and Smith performed in Dave Clark & Friends for a few more years. Smith began writing jingles and picking up session work. He can be heard on the original cast album of *Evita* and a 1990 album of his own music and rock classics. Clark wrote and produced the musical *Time*, which premiered in 1986.

PETULA CLARK

Petula Clark broke all of the unwritten rules of the British Invasion, save one: she was British. Clark came to rock success as a solo artist in the age of bands, as a woman in an era dominated by male sounds, and at the ripe old age of thirty-two. She appeared on the U.S. scene in 1964, during the first wave of the Invasion, with "Downtown." The song hit #1 in the U.S. and won her a Grammy for Best Rock and Roll Single. In 1965 she toured the U.S., making appearances at major clubs throughout the country, as well as on the TV shows of Ed Sullivan, Dean Martin, and Andy Williams. Clark released numerous records, landing some fifteen in the Top 40, including "I Know a Place" and "Don't Sleep in the Subway." By the late sixties she had returned to an acting career that she began as a child, filming *Goodbye, Mr. Chips* and *Finian's Rainbow*. Making her Broadway debut with *Blood Brothers* in 1993, Clark continues to perform and record.

THE SPENCER DAVIS GROUP

Although The Spencer Davis Group never found the fame that came to The Beatles, The Rolling Stones, and other British Invasion bands, they are now hailed as one of the most influential bands of the era. This was the band that the better-known Invasion bands went to hear when not performing themselves. The Spencer Davis Group was formed by a professor of German who played a little music on the side. Davis (vocals, guitar, and harmonica) left his university job in 1963 to tour England with drummer Pete York, vocalist/guitarist/keyboardist Steve Winwood, and bassist Muff Winwood (brother of Steve). The group played with a gritty, driving R&B style that scored them a few quick hits, including "Gimme Some Lovin' " in late 1966 and "I'm a Man" in 1967. Steve Winwood moved on in 1967, creating Traffic. Muff became a producer. Eventually Davis added Nigel Olsson and Dee Murray, but when Murray left to sign on with Elton John in 1969, The Spencer Davis Group folded. Davis never returned to the classroom. He has maintained a busy performing career and heads a management firm in L.A.

GERRY & THE PACEMAKERS

For a time, Gerry & The Pacemakers ran on a parallel course with The Beatles. A Liverpool skiffle band, formed in 1959, The Pacemakers consisted of Gerry Marsden on vocals and guitar, Les Maguire on piano, John Chadwick on bass, and Freddie Marsden on drums. Gerry & The Pacemakers were the second group, after The Beatles, to be signed by manager Brian Epstein, sharing producer George Martin with the Fab Four as well. The group scored #1 hits in Britain with their first three singles. Like The Beatles, they played "The Ed Sullivan Show" in 1964, snagging an American following immediately with "Don't Let the Sun Catch You Crying." Their rendition of "How Do You Do It?" first recorded by The Beatles, hit #9 in the U.S. in 1964. "Ferry 'Cross the Mersey" (referring to the Mersey River, which runs through Liverpool and from which the Merseybeat took its name) made it into the U.S. Top 10 in 1965. Marsden wrote a number of original songs for the film of the same name. The group soon began to falter, finally breaking up in 1967. Marsden put together a touring version of The Pacemakers in 1973 to play a nostalgia tour of the U.S. and continues to perform throughout the world.

HERMAN'S HERMITS

Herman's Hermits came together in Manchester, England, in 1963. Members Peter "Herman" Noone on vocals and piano, Karl Green on guitar and harmonica, Keith Hopwood on guitar, Derek "Lek" Leckenby on guitar, and Barry Whitwam on drums managed to put eleven songs onto the Top 10 charts between 1964 and 1967. Group leader Peter Noone apparently bore a resemblance to the character Sherman on the "Rocky and Bullwinkle" television cartoon. The name Sherman was shortened to Herman and stuck with him. Before changing styles relegated them to the back burner, the band appeared in *Where the Boys Meet the Girls*, with Connie Francis. The band split up in 1971, battling over royalties to such hits as "I'm Into Something Good" (1964), "Mrs. Brown You've Got a Lovely Daughter" (1965), and "There's a Kind of Hush" (1967). One of their most memorable hits was "I'm Henry VIII, I Am" (1965), which was written in 1911. Noone later reunited the band for several rock nostalgia television shows. Jimmy Page and John Paul Jones (later of Led Zeppelin) can be heard playing on several of the band's hits. The band has come back together on several occasions both with and without "Herman."

The Hollies

The Hollies' three-part harmonies and distinctive guitar sounds made them one of the biggest commercial successes of the British Invasion bands. Like most of the British bands, The Hollies began by covering early rock and R&B tunes. They eventually began recording original material, written by their own members and others, scoring a long string of hits. Members included vocalist and guitarist Graham Nash, guitarist Anthony Hicks, vocalist Allan Clarke, drummer Donald Rathbone (later replaced by Robert Elliott), and bassist Eric Haydock. Nash and Clarke were childhood buddies who formed the earlier groups The Two Teens, Ricky & Dane, and The Guytones. They finally made it as The Hollies, hitting the U.S. Top 10 with "Bus Stop" (1966). That year also saw the hit "Stop Stop Stop." With time, their music grew more sophisticated, eventually moving into the psychedelic genre. Haydock left in 1966, replaced by Bernard Calvert. Nash departed in 1968, forming Crosby, Stills & Nash. The band carried on, replacing Nash with Terry Sylvester and racking up such successes as "He Ain't Heavy...He's My Brother" (1970), "Long Cool Woman (In a Black Dress)" (1972), and "The Air That I Breathe" (1974). Clarke left in 1971, returned in 1973, and quit again in 1977. The group issued their last recording, *Buddy Holly*, in 1980. Nash, Clarke, Elliott, and Hicks reunited in 1983 to record *What Goes Around....* In 1988 the band placed a reissue of "He Ain't Heavy...He's My Brother" at the top of the British charts. Clarke, Hicks, and Elliott were still touring well into the nineties.

The Kinks

Although The Kinks lived in the shadow of The Beatles and The Rolling Stones, the band was one of the most influential of the early British Invasion. Sloppy musicianship and on-stage arguments didn't prevent the group from outlasting all other contenders to British Invasion fame. Soon after Ray Davies joined brother Dave's band The Ravens in 1963, the group began to change. The band, with Ray and Dave on vocals and guitars, Mick Avory on drums, and Pete Quaife on drums, changed its name to The Kinks and turned out a few unsuccessful singles. The group hit pay dirt with "You Really Got Me" (1964), taking it to #1 in Britain and #10 in the U.S. They followed it with the huge success "Tired of Waiting for You" (1965), which made #1 in Britain and #7 in the U.S. Following their 1965 tour of the U.S, the group was banned from the country until 1969 for reasons of "unprofessional conduct." The group garnered international attention at the end of the sixties and, with a few personnel changes, continued scoring hits, including "Come Dancing" (1983). The band was inducted into the Rock and Roll Hall of Fame in 1990. In 1993 the group toured the U.S. for the first time in several years. In an amazing example of survival, the group continues to perform and record in the late nineties.

BILLY J. KRAMER WITH THE DAKOTAS

Manager Brian Epstein, famous for his work with The Beatles, heard Billy J. Kramer in one audition and The Dakotas in another. The Dakotas were a skiffle-turned-R&B band featuring Mike Maxfield on lead guitar, Robin Macdonald on rhythm guitar, Raymond Jones on bass, and Tony Mansfield on drums. Finding potential in both acts, Epstein put them together and set them up with a couple of songs by the songwriting team of John Lennon and Paul McCartney, creating one of the best bands of the initial British Invasion wave. The group shared both Epstein and producer George Martin with The Beatles. Lennon and McCartney's "Do You Want to Know a Secret" was the group's first hit. The group mounted a U.S. tour in 1964, scoring hits in the States that year with such tunes as "Bad to Me," "From a Window," and "Little Children," which became one of the ten best-selling singles in the U.S. in 1964. The group continued to record through 1964 and 1965, disbanding in 1966. Kramer (born William Ashton) continued recording as a solo artist in Britain. In 1984 he surfaced in Long Island, New York, and continues to perform a nostalgia act.

THE MINDBENDERS (WAYNE FONTANA & THE MINDBENDERS)

Singer Glyn Geoffrey Ellis and his band, the Jets, were scheduled to play for a Fontana Records talent scout in 1963. When only Ellis and bass player Bob Lang turned up to play, they recruited two musicians in attendance, guitarist Eric Stewart and drummer Ric Rothwell, to bail them out. The group won a contract and quickly borrowed the record label's name, dubbing Ellis "Wayne Fontana." The group then pulled its own name from a British horror film. After recording a few R&B covers in 1963, Wayne Fontana & The Mindbenders hit the British charts with "Um, Um, Um, Um, Um, Um" in 1964. The group scored an international hit in 1965 with "The Game of Love," after which Fontana decided to go solo. The Mindbenders, minus Fontana, landed "A Groovy Kind of Love" and "Ashes to Ashes" on the U.S. charts in 1966, but public interest in the band soon waned. After appearing in the movie *To Sir, With Love*, the group disbanded. A reconstituted version of Wayne Fontana and The Mindbenders is still performing.

The Moody Blues

The Moody Blues, formed in 1964, was one of the most innovative forces in rock during the late sixties. The group initially found success during the British Invasion with "Go Now" (1965), their second single. Band members Denny Laine on guitar and vocals, Mike Pinder on keyboards and vocals, Ray Thomas on flute and vocals, Clint Warwick on bass, and Graham Edge on drums took the single to #1 in the U.K. and #10 in the U.S. Over the next few years the band experimented with their sound, eventually releasing the groundbreaking album *Days of Future Passed* (1967), with musicians of the London Festival Orchestra. Combining rock and classical sounds, the album featured Justin Hayward (replacing Laine) and John Lodge (replacing Warwick). Audiences left in the lurch by a slow-down in production from The Beatles and The Rolling Stones turned the heavily orchestrated album—with its notable singles "Nights in White Satin" and "Tuesday Afternoon"—into an international hit. It was followed in 1968 by *In Search of the Lost Chord*, a psychedelic ode to mysticism, drugs, and Timothy Leary, recorded by overdubbing synthesized orchestrations on a Mellotron (a keyboard instrument that played tape recordings of instrument sounds). A few more overdubbed albums and the group began to realize that they could no longer re-create their recorded performances in live concerts. In 1970 they released *A Question of Balance*, featuring music that was suitable for live performance. The Moody Blues maintained a following long after the British Invasion years ended, despite critical accusations of a pretentious and bombastic style. They released a steady flow of albums throughout the seventies and eighties, retaining a style that had long ceased to be cutting-edge, but continued to sell. *A Night at Red Rocks with the Colorado Symphony Orchestra* (1993) reflected the group's successful latter-day performances with regional orchestras, in which they re-created the grandiose sounds of their studio days. A four-CD retrospective boxed set entitled *Time Traveller* was released in 1994.

Peter & Gordon

Had Paul McCartney not set his cap for Peter Asher's sister, Peter & Gordon (Asher and Gordon Waller) might never have had their big break. McCartney wrote "World without Love" for the duo, presumably to impress sister Jane, and in 1964 Peter & Gordon took it to the British Top 10 and then to the U.S. In the end it ranked as one of the year's most successful singles. The duo toured the U.S., appearing on the "The Ed Sullivan Show." They later returned to the States and appeared on most of the then-popular rock TV shows. Their hits included "I Go to Pieces" and "True Love Ways" (both 1965). The duo split up in the late sixties when Asher moved on to manage The Beatles' new record company, Apple Records. It was Asher who signed the young James Taylor while still in London and propelled the singer toward superstar status in the seventies. Asher soon moved to L.A. to head one of the major talent agencies in the country. Gordon Waller apparently left the music industry.

Procol Harum

A melody borrowed from J.S. Bach and mystical lyrics by Keith Reid created the first of two U.S. hits for Procol Harum, "A Whiter Shade of Pale" (1967). The second came in 1972 with an orchestrated version of "Conquistador." Like The Moody Blues, Procol Harum was known as a classical rock band. The group traced its roots back to 1963 and an R&B band called The Paramounts, featuring Gary Brooker, Robin Trower, Chris Copping, and B.J. Wilson. The group broke up in 1966, the same year Brooker and Keith Reid (who never performed but was always listed as a member of the band) put together Procol Harum. The new band included Brooker on piano and vocals, Reid as lyricist, Matthew Fisher on organ, Ray Royer on guitar, Dave Knights on bass, and Bobby Harrison on drums. Royer and Harrison were soon replaced by original Paramounts members Trower and Wilson, who recorded the first three albums with the group. When Fisher and Knights quit the band in 1969, Copping returned to the fold. After the successful album *Procol Harum Live: In Concert with the Edmonton Symphony Orchestra & The Da Camera Singers*, the group began heading into a guitar-driven style that never quite worked. After several more personnel changes, they took a two-year hiatus, finally disbanding after recording *Something Magic* (1977). Back together in 1991, the group recorded *The Prodigal Stranger*, with yet a few more personnel changes. Brooker has continued to perform and record, starting work in 1994 on an album entitled *Symphonic Music of Procol Harum*.

The Rolling Stones

The Rolling Stones came to the British Invasion with the cultivated image of bad boys. They grew into that image, thanks in large part to lead singer Mick Jagger's flagrant half-nude on-stage antics, lyrics about sex and drugs, and songs like "Sympathy for the Devil." With Mick Jagger on vocals, Keith Richards on guitar and vocals, Brian Jones on guitar, Bill Wyman on bass, and Charlie Watts on drums, the group's sound was typically hard-driving and raucous, as typified early on by such hits as "Time Is on My Side" (1964) and "(I Can't Get No) Satisfaction" (1965). Richards was the musical genius behind the group, sharing credit with Jagger for a long list of songs like "Angie," "Beast of Burden," "Honky Tonk Women," "It's Only Rock 'n' Roll (But I Like It)," and "You Can't Always Get What You Want." The band's on-stage anarchy was a group effort, spearheaded by Jagger. Brian Jones, who had become a less and less vital element of the group over time, left the band in June 1969, only to drown a month later. He was replaced by Mick Taylor. Taylor left in 1975 and was replaced by Ron Wood. By the late seventies, The Stones had gone disco, with a couple of forgettable albums in the doomed genre. By the eighties they had become a stadium band, playing their former hits to faithful audiences. The latter-day Stones continued to record and tour sporadically in the early nineties, faced with criticism for their multi-million-dollar shows and apathetic recordings. In 1992 original member Bill Wyman left the group after thirty years and was replaced by hired gun Darryl Jones. The band released *Voodoo Lounge* in 1994, which made it to #2 on the charts. Fans and critics alike praised the album, and it won The Stones the Grammy for Best Rock Album of 1994. Throughout the years, group members have made successful solo ventures in various genres. The group's career has been the perfect parallel of rock music's mutation from the rebellious sounds of youth to lucrative big business.

The Searchers

With a more refined, carefully harmonized sound than most Liverpool pop-rock groups, The Searchers were one of the best post-Beatles bands to come out of Liverpool. Founded in 1957 as a skiffle band, the group moved to pop-rock as Johnny Sandon & The Searchers. Sandon left in early 1962, leaving John McNally and Mike Pender on guitar and vocals, Tony Jackson on bass and vocals, and Chris Curtis on drums and vocals. The band scored their first British hit in 1963 with "Sweets for My Sweet." "Needles and Pins" (1964) made it to #1 in Britain and #13 in the U.S. The group's following U.S. hits that year were "Don't Throw Your Love Away" and "Love Potion Number 9." They continued to score hits in Britain throughout 1965, moving to cabaret clubs when the pop world's fascination with Liverpool began to dwindle. After replacing Jackson with Frank Allen and Curtis with John Blunt and then Blunt with Billy Adamson, they continued to perform and record, adding new material that kept them from being relegated to nostalgia-band status. The album *Second Take* appeared in 1972, followed by *Sire* in 1979. *Love's Melodies* appeared in 1981, with Spencer James replacing Pender. The group was touring well into the eighties, playing to large crowds in the U.S. Mike Pender moved on to form Mike Pender's Searchers. Both groups of Searchers have done considerable touring.

The Seekers

The Seekers hailed not from Liverpool but from Down Under. The soft-rock group was noted for good tunes and creative harmonies. Original members included Athol Guy on bass, Keith Potger on guitar, Bruce Woodley on guitar, and Judith Durham on vocals. Their mid-sixties hits included "I'll Never Find Another You" (1965) and "Georgy Girl" (1966), which was nominated for an Oscar as the title song of the film by the same name. Although The Seekers parted company in 1968, Keith Potger appeared with The New Seekers shortly thereafter. The New Seekers are best known for the hits "Look What They've Done to My Song Ma" (1970) and "I'd Like to Teach the World to Sing (In Perfect Harmony)" (1971).

Dusty Springfield

One of Britain's best-selling pop-rock singers of the sixties, Dusty Springfield found her way to the U.S. pop charts as a solo act. Born Mary O'Brien, Springfield and her brother Tom were part of the folk-pop trio The Springfields before she struck out on her own. Singing in a husky voice, by the end of the sixties she had racked up seventeen hits in Britain and ten in the U.S. Her best-known songs included "I Only Want to Be with You" and "Wishin' and Hopin' " (both 1964). In 1969 her blue-eyed-soul album *Dusty in Memphis* garnered critical praise. Springfield made a comeback hit in 1987 with "What Have I Done to Deserve This?" which reached #2 in both the U.S. and the U.K. Her 1990 album *Reputation* made the British Top 20. She was still recording in the mid nineties.

The Troggs

The Troggs caught the British Invasion already in full swing, scoring their first U.S. hit with "Wild Thing" (1966). Other 1966 hits included "With a Girl Like You" and "I Can't Control Myself." Original members Reg Presley on vocals, Chris Britton on lead guitar, Peter Staples on bass, and Ronnie Bond on drums landed one more song in the Top 10 in early 1968: "Love Is All Around." But they found the band's popularity fading. Staples left at that point and the group soon disbanded. The Troggs reappeared in 1972 with new members Richard Moore on guitar and Tony Murray on bass. The band has managed to keep a loyal following in Britain well into the nineties, where their music is heard on television and their greatest hits are frequently used in commercials. In 1992 the group played at rocker Sting's wedding.

THE WHO

Roger Daltrey's shouting voice, Pete Townshend's power chords, and Keith Moon's unpredictable, flamboyant drum antics gave The Who its signature sound and style. Original members were Townshend on guitar and vocals; Daltrey on vocals; John Entwistle on bass, French horn, and vocals; and Dougie Sandon on drums (soon replaced by Keith Moon). During a mid-sixties gig, Townshend snapped the neck of his guitar on a low ceiling. Furious, he smashed the instrument to bits. When the audience seemed to love it, Keith Moon began to attack his drum kit. An act was born. First known as The Detours and later The Numbers, the group was explaining to their manager, on the night of the first smashed instruments, that they wanted to go back to their earlier title The Detours. He said, "The who?" The band agreed, "That's right, The Who." The Who's high-energy, driving style won them hits with "My Generation" (1966) and "I Can See for Miles" (1967). *Tommy* (1969) brought rock opera to the world. The group effectively ended in 1978 at Keith Moon's death from an overdose of medication he was taking to help with alcohol withdrawal. They continued to perform and record, but they agreed that without Moon something was missing. Tragedy struck again in 1979 while The Who was playing the Cincinnati Riverfront Coliseum. Eleven concertgoers were killed when the doors were opened and the crowd rushed for prime seats. By the late eighties, Townshend was performing behind a Plexiglas sound shield to protect the remnants of his damaged hearing. The alcohol and drug use that killed Moon nearly did Townshend in as well. Although the group broke up in 1982, they have reassembled over the years for various performances, including a forty-two-stop tour of the U.S. in 1989. *Tommy* has found a life of its own, including a run on Broadway, for which it won five Tony Awards in 1993, including Best Score.

THE YARDBIRDS

The Yardbirds were one of the most influential bands in rock, making their greatest contribution with innovative guitar work. Founded as The Most Blueswailing Yardbirds in 1963, the group introduced three of rock's best guitarists: Eric Clapton, Jimmy Page, and Jeff Beck. Original members included Keith Relf on vocals and harmonica, Chris Dreja on guitar, Jim McCarty on drums, Paul Samwell-Smith on bass, and Anthony "Top" Topham (soon replaced by Eric Clapton) on guitar. Clapton saw the group through its early years with hits like "For Your Love" (1965). He left in 1965 because he felt the band was becoming too commercial and pop-oriented. In stepped Jeff Beck, who began to experiment with guitar effects, introducing the sounds of feedback and fuzz. At this point The Yardbirds scored a Top 20 hit by reviving the Bo Diddley classic "I'm a Man." Jimmy Page then arrived to replace Samwell-Smith on bass. The moment Dreja mastered the bass, Page joined Beck as co-lead guitarist for a brief time before Beck, too, left the group. The band lasted only a short time with Page on lead, breaking up in 1968. McCarty and Relf continued to perform together in the groups Together, Renaissance, and Armageddon. Relf died in 1976. Dreja eventually became a photographer. Page created The New Yardbirds to meet contract obligations of the original group, eventually changing the group's name to Led Zeppelin. McCarty, Dreja, and Samwell-Smith reunited in 1983, eventually forming a band called Box of Frogs. McCarty joined the British Invasion All-Stars in 1989 and has since recorded with the New Age ensemble Stairway.

BITS AND PIECES

Words and Music by DAVE CLARK
and MIKE SMITH

BUS STOP

Words and Music by
GRAHAM GOULDMAN

CARRIE-ANNE

Words and Music by ALLAN CLARKE,
TONY HICKS and GRAHAM NASH

A DAY IN THE LIFE

Words and Music by JOHN LENNON
and PAUL McCARTNEY

DON'T BRING ME DOWN

Words and Music by GERRY GOFFIN
and CAROLE KING

Moderate rock tempo

8va lower - - - - - - -

loco

1. 3. When you com-plain and crit-i-cize__ I feel I'm noth-ing in your eyes,__

2. Sac-ri-fi - ces I will make,__ I'm read-y to give as well as take,__

It makes me feel like giv-in' up__ be-cause my best just ain't good e-nough,__

One thing I need is your re-spect,__ One thing I can't take is your ne-glect,__

DON'T LET ME BE MISUNDERSTOOD

Words and Music by BENNIE BENJAMIN,
SOL MARCUS and GLORIA CALDWELL

FERRY 'CROSS THE MERSEY

Words and Music by
GERARD MARSDEN

With a beat

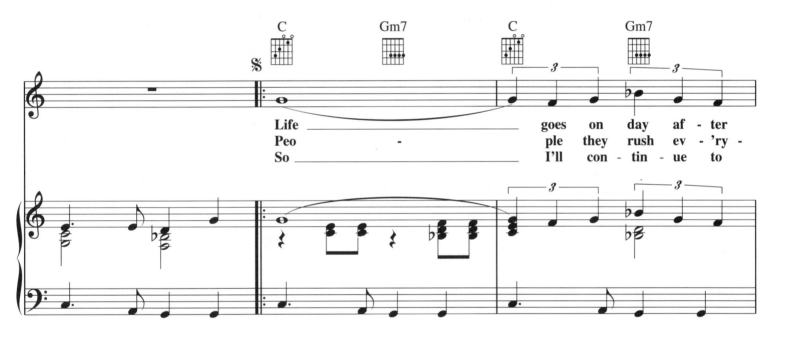

Life _____ goes on day af - ter
Peo - ple they rush ev - 'ry -
So _____ I'll con - tin - ue to

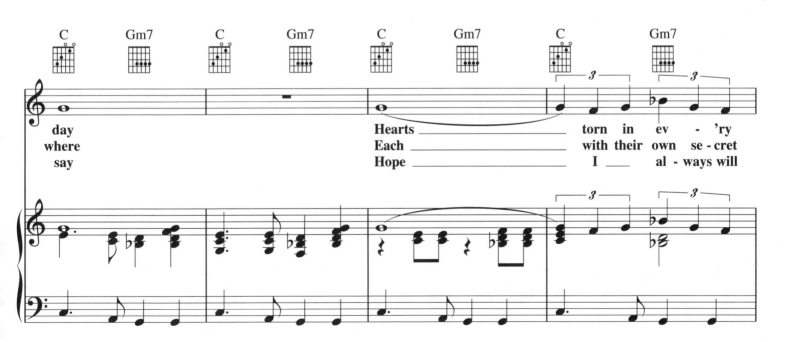

day Hearts _____ torn in ev - 'ry
where Each _____ with their own se - cret
say Hope _____ I ___ al - ways will

DON'T LET THE SUN CATCH YOU CRYING

Words and Music by GERARD MARSDEN, FRED MARSDEN,
LES CHADWICK and LES MAGUIRE

FROM A WINDOW

Words and Music by JOHN LENNON
and PAUL McCARTNEY

GEORGY GIRL

Words by JIM DALE
Music by TOM SPRINGFIELD

GIMME SOME LOVIN'

Words and Music by SPENCER DAVIS,
MUFF WINWOOD and STEVE WINWOOD

GLAD ALL OVER

Words and Music by DAVE CLARK
and MIKE SMITH

GO NOW

Words and Music by MILTON BENNETT
and LARRY BANKS

A GROOVY KIND OF LOVE

Words and Music by TONI WINE
and CAROLE BAYER SAGER

Repeat and fade

A HARD DAY'S NIGHT

Words and Music by JOHN LENNON
and PAUL McCARTNEY

I GO TO PIECES

By DEL SHANNON

HOW DO YOU DO IT?

Words and Music by
MITCH MURRAY

I CAN SEE FOR MILES

Words and Music by
PETER TOWNSHEND

I know you've de-ceived me. Now here's a sur-prise.

I know that you have 'cos there's ma - gic in_____ my

eyes. I can see for miles and miles and

I KNOW A PLACE

Words and Music by
TONY HATCH

I'LL NEVER FIND ANOTHER YOU

Words and Music by
TOM SPRINGFIELD

82

I ONLY WANT TO BE WITH YOU

Words and Music by MIKE HAWKER
and IVOR RAYMONDE

I WANT TO HOLD YOUR HAND

Words and Music by JOHN LENNON
and PAUL McCARTNEY

MCA music publishing

I'M A MAN

By ELLAS McDANIEL

I'M A MAN

Words and Music by JIMMY MILLER
and STEVE WINWOOD

Lyrics:

Well, my pad is ver-y mes-sy, got the whis-kers on my chin.
got to keep my im-age while sus-pend-ed on a throne that looks

Nev-er had no prob-lems 'cause I al-ways pay the rent.   I've
out up-on a king-dom filled with peo-ple all un-known, who im-

got no time for lov-in' 'cause my time is all used up;   I
ag-ine I'm not hu-man and my heart is made of stone, And I

I'M INTO SOMETHING GOOD

Words and Music by GERRY GOFFIN
and CAROLE KING

LOVE POTION NUMBER 9

Words and Music by JERRY LEIBER
and MIKE STOLLER

LOVE IS ALL AROUND

Words and Music by
REG PRESLEY

Got-ta keep it mov-ing. _____ Ooh, it's writ-ten in __ the wind, __ oh, __

_____ ev-'ry-where I go. ____ So __

if you real-ly love me, love me, love me, come on and let it show. _____

Repeat and Fade

____ Come on and let it show. _ Come on __ and let it show. _

MARIE

Words and Music by
IRVING BERLIN

MISERY

Words and Music by JOHN LENNON
and PAUL McCARTNEY

MRS. BROWN YOU'VE GOT A LOVELY DAUGHTER

Words and Music by
TREVOR PEACOCK

Tell her that I'm well and feel - in' fine;

Don't let on, Don't say she's broke my heart,

I'd go down on my knees, but it's no good to pine.

Repeat and Fade

Mis - sis Brown you've got a love - ly daugh - ter.

MY GENERATION

Words and Music by
PETER TOWNSHEND

ON A CAROUSEL

Words and Music by TONY HICKS,
GRAHAM NASH and ALLAN CLARKE

Flowing rock tempo

SAN FRANCISCAN NIGHTS

Words and Music by BARRY JENKINS, DANNY McCULLOCH,
JOHNNY WEIDER and VIC BRAGGS

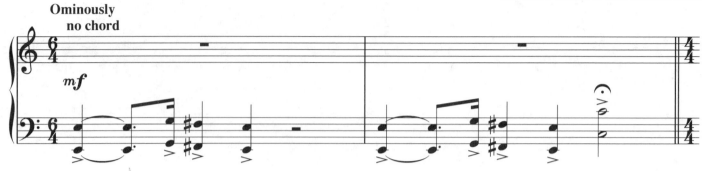

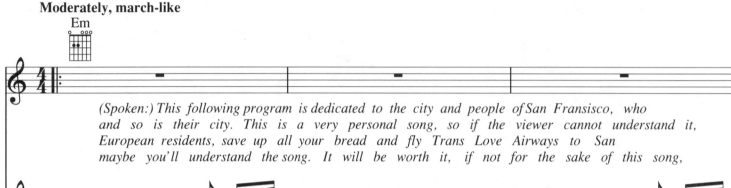

Moderately, march-like

Em

(Spoken:) This following program is dedicated to the city and people of San Fransisco, who
and so is their city. This is a very personal song, so if the viewer cannot understand it,
European residents, save up all your bread and fly Trans Love Airways to San
maybe you'll understand the song. It will be worth it, if not for the sake of this song,

Play 4 times

Moderate Rock

C   Em/B

may not know it, but they are beautiful,
particularly those of you who are
Fransico, U.S.A.   Then
but for the sake of your own peace of mind.

San Fran - cis - co.

D.S. and Fade

STOP STOP STOP

Words and Music by ALLAN CLARKE,
TONY HICKS and GRAHAM NASH

Can't they un - der - stand __ that I want her hap - pens ev - 'ry

week. Heav - y hand up - on __ my __ col - lar

throws me in the street Stop stop

Ab

stop all the danc - ing give me time to breathe

Bb

THERE'S A KIND OF HUSH
(All Over the World)

Words and Music by LES REED
and GEOFF STEPHENS

TICKET TO RIDE

Words and Music by JOHN LENNON
and PAUL McCARTNEY

TIME IS ON MY SIDE

Words and Music by
JERRY RAGOVOY

Time _____ is on my side. _____ (Spoken:) Yes, it is!

Time _____ is on my side. _____ (Spoken:) Yes, it is!

TRUE LOVE WAYS

Words and Music by NORMAN PETTY
and BUDDY HOLLY

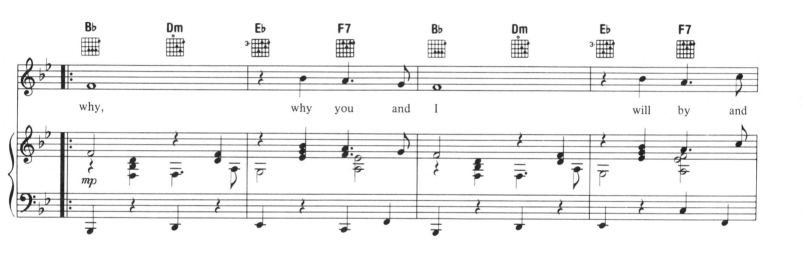

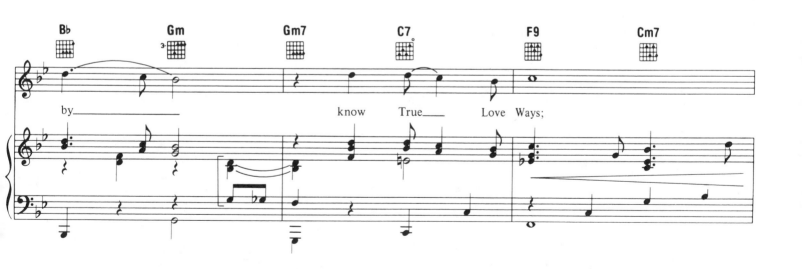

WE CAN WORK IT OUT

Words and Music by JOHN LENNON
and PAUL McCARTNEY

A WHITER SHADE OF PALE

Words and Music by KEITH REID
and GARY BROOKER

We skipped the light fan - dan - go, _____ turned cart - wheels 'cross the
She said, "I'm home _____ on shore leave," _____ though in truth we _____ were at
She said, "There is _____ no rea - son, _____ and the truth is _____ plain to

floor; _____ I was feel - ing kind of sea - sick,
sea; _____ So I took her by the look - ing glass
see," _____ But I wan - dered through my play - ing cards

WE GOTTA GET OUT OF THIS PLACE

Words and Music by BARRY MANN
and CYNTHIA WEIL

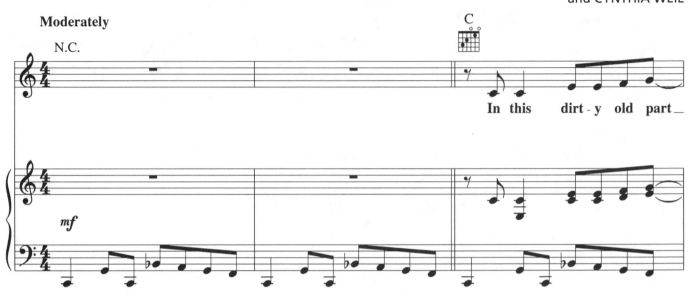

My little girl, you're so young and pretty.

And one thing I know is true: you'll be dead before your time is through.

See my daddy in bed. He's dyin'. You know, his hair is turn-

WILD THING

Words and Music by
CHIP TAYLOR

162

WILD THING,

You make my heart sing.

You make eve - ry - thing ___ groov - y. ___

Repeat and Fade

WILD THING.

WILLOW WEEP FOR ME

Words and Music by
ANN RONELL

WISHIN' AND HOPIN'

Lyric by HAL DAVID
Music by BURT BACHARACH

WORLD WITHOUT LOVE

Words and Music by JOHN LENNON
and PAUL McCARTNEY

YOU REALLY GOT ME

Words and Music by
RAY DAVIES

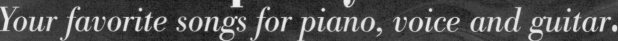